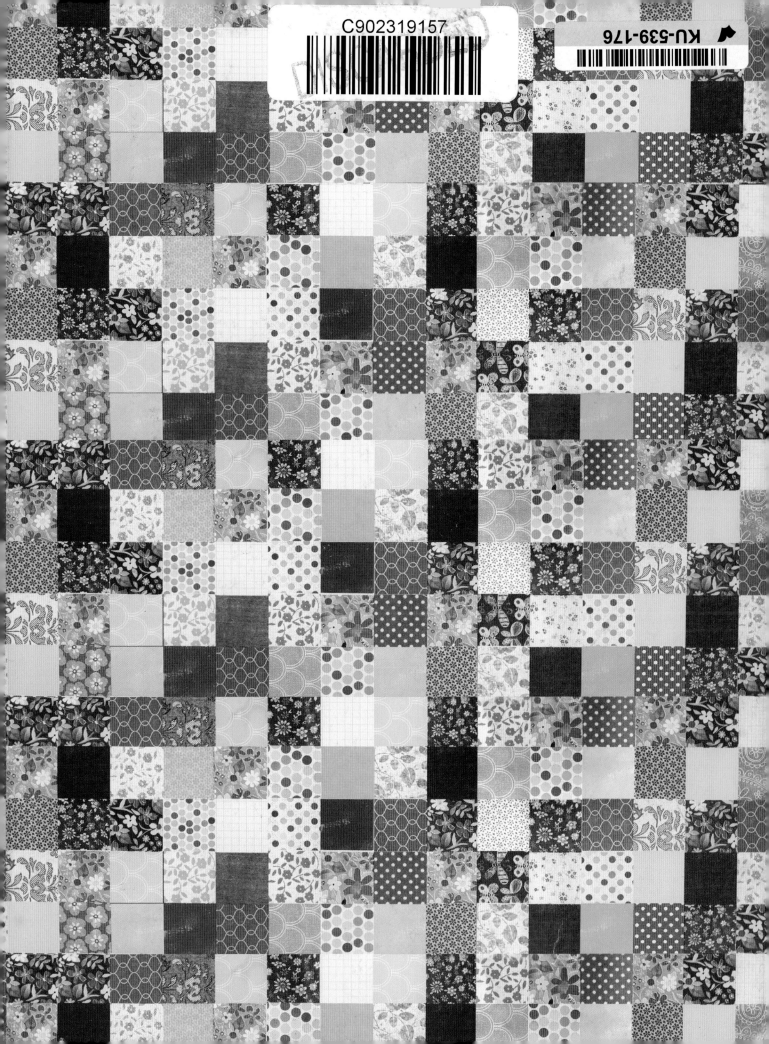

Crafty
Gifts

Jane Bull

DK

Design and text Jane Bull
Photographer Andy Crawford
Editor Violet Peto
Design Assistant Eleanor Bates
Producer, Pre-Production Nikoleta Parasaki
Producer John Casey
Jacket Designer Amy Keast
Jacket Coordinator Francesca Young
Managing Editor Penny Smith
Managing Art Editor Mabel Chan
Publisher Mary Ling
Art Director Jane Bull

This book is for my sister
Margaret

First published in Great Britain in 2017 by
Dorling Kindersley Limited
80 Strand, London WC2R 0RL

Copyright © 2017 Dorling Kindersley Limited
A Penguin Random House Company
10 9 8 7 6 5 4 3 2 1
001–297035–Oct/2017

A CIP catalogue record for this book
is available from the British Library.
ISBN: 978-0-2412-7580-1

Printed and bound in China

A WORLD OF IDEAS:
SEE ALL THERE IS TO KNOW

www.dk.com

Safety
Projects in this book may require adult
supervision.
**When you see the warning triangle, take extra
care and ask an adult for help.**

Contents

Crafty kit

It's good to be prepared, so keep these items handy. They will be needed for most of the projects that follow. Additional materials you will need are suggested throughout the book.

Glue stick

For paper and card

Scissors

Sticky tape

Strong glue

An all-purpose strong glue will stick to fabric and plastic.

Felt-tip pen

Colourful paper and card

Pencil

Ruler

Crafty gift ideas

Gems

Beads and
buttons

Snowman

Santa

Festive
trees

Tiny jingle
bells

**You will
need:**

Sewing needle
with large eye
and blunt end

Thick cotton
thread

30cm (12in)

Button charms

These colourful gems make perfect gifts at festive times. Enjoy them hanging on the Christmas tree or sparkling against a sunny window.

1
Thread the needle, and pass it through the buttons and beads.

2
Then pass the needle back through a different hole.

3
Make the threads equal lengths and knot the ends together.

Icicle

Mix up the buttons and beads to create different colourways and dangly shapes.

Salt dough treasures

Make fancy decorations, colourful frames, and gift tags using salt dough. Shape it, bake it, and paint for a luscious finish, and transform simple salt dough into these special presents.

You will need:

300g (10oz) plain flour

+

100g (3½oz) salt

+

1 tsp cooking oil

+

200ml (7fl oz) water

=

Make some dough

Pour all the ingredients into a mixing bowl, then mix them together with your hands until you can make a ball.

You will need:

Candle holders

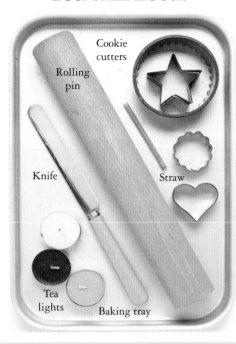

Rolling pin

Cookie cutters

Knife

Straw

Tea lights

Baking tray

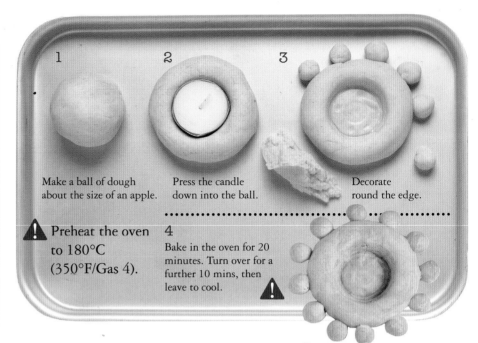

1 Make a ball of dough about the size of an apple.

2 Press the candle down into the ball.

3 Decorate round the edge.

⚠ **Preheat the oven to 180°C (350°F/Gas 4).**

4 Bake in the oven for 20 minutes. Turn over for a further 10 mins, then leave to cool. ⚠

Paint and decorate

Make sure the items are completely cold before painting. Mix acrylic paint with PVA glue. This will create a thick coat of paint and add a sheen to your work.

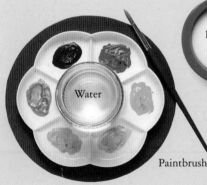

Water

Acrylic paints

Paintbrush

PVA glue

Apply the paint. Add more coats if necessary.

Shape before you bake

Pull out the sides of the dough by pinching it.

Make cuts round the edge with a knife.

Make shapes round the edge with a fork.

Bowl

Ovenproof bowl

Rolling pin

Salt dough mixture

Knife

Baking tray

⚠ **Preheat the oven to 180°C (350°F/Gas 4).**

Sprinkle flour on board.

1 Roll out the dough to 5mm (¼in) thickness.

Pick up the dough on the rolling pin.

2 Drape the dough over the bowl.

3 Cut away the extra dough.

Decorations

Preheat the oven to 180°C (350°F/Gas 4). ⚠️

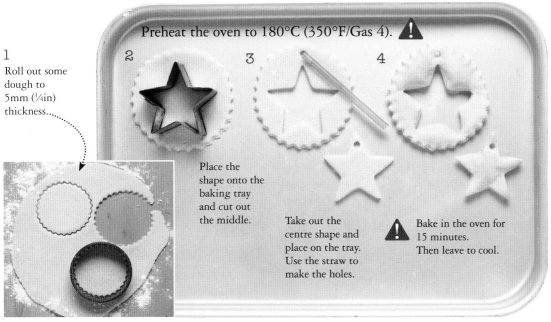

1 Roll out some dough to 5mm (¼in) thickness.

2

3

4

Place the shape onto the baking tray and cut out the middle.

Take out the centre shape and place on the tray. Use the straw to make the holes.

⚠️ Bake in the oven for 15 minutes. Then leave to cool.

Baking tips: ⚠️

• Heat the oven before baking.

• Make the dough shapes directly on the tray because they may become misshapen if moved.

• You may need to bake for longer as the dough needs to dry out properly.

Paint the decorations. Leave to dry and add other colours.

Add a photo

1 Place the decoration over the photo. Draw round the edge.

2 Cut out the photo slightly smaller than the outer edge.

3 Spread glue on the back of the decoration and position the photo.

Leave glue to dry, then attach ribbons.

For extra decoration, you will also need:
• photo
• ribbon

⚠️ Bake in the oven for 25 minutes or until the dough has dried out.

4 Roll out a sausage shape with the extra dough. Place the sausage on the base of the bowl.

5 Leave to cool before painting.

6 Paint inside and outside the bowl. Allow to dry and paint on colourful patterns.

Apple packs

Make a great crop of crafty gifts from recycled plastic bottles. Choose any size or colour and transform them into these clever, apple-shaped containers.

How to make an apple pack

You will need:

• two plastic bottles • some goodies to pack inside
• green or red tissue paper • ribbon • scissors
• green and brown paper • pencil • strong glue

A clear bottle with a red tissue paper apple

1

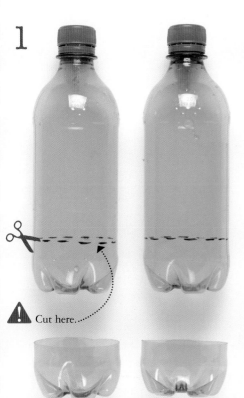

Cut here.

2

Wrap up your gift in green or red tissue paper.

3

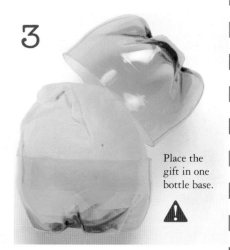

Place the gift in one bottle base.

4

Push the two bottle bases together.

Glue on ribbon to decorate.

5 Cut out leaves in different sizes.

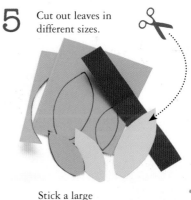

Stick a large leaf on first.

Then stick the base of the stalk on top.

6 Now make the stalk and add the leaves.

Cut a strip of brown paper 10cm x 1½cm (4in x ¾in) for the stalk.

Fold twice to make a base.

Put glue on both ends.

Glue the two ends together with a leaf in between.

DIY gingerbread folk

This clever kit makes a great gift for a keen cook who loves to bake. Pack up the ingredients into a fancy jar, then attach a cookie cutter and instructions on how to make these delicious gingerbread treats.

You will need:

• Spoon • Clean paper

200g (7oz) plain flour

1 tsp ground ginger and 1tsp mixed spice

1 tsp bicarbonate of soda

100g (3½oz) dark brown sugar

100g (3½oz) icing sugar

A clean, 1-litre (1¾-pint) jar with a lid

Ribbon

Gingerbread cookie cutter and card tag (with instructions on reverse)

Plastic bag filled with candy-coated sweets for decoration

Plastic bag for the icing sugar

How to fill the jar

1 Spoon in the flour and bicarbonate of soda.

Make a paper funnel to stop the flour from spilling.

2 Add sugar, then spice.

Press each layer down with the back of a spoon.

3 Add a bag of icing sugar.

This way the icing sugar won't get mixed up with the other ingredients.

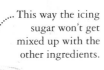

4 Screw on the lid.

Pop in a bag of sweets to decorate the biscuits.

Instructions

Write the instructions on a piece of card and attach it to the jar.

How to cook your cookies

Makes: 18 gingerbread folk
You will also need:
• 100g (3½oz) butter • 1 egg
• 2 tbsp golden syrup
For the icing: lemon juice
Equipment: mixing bowl, wooden spoon, cling film, rolling pin, baking tray, small bowl, cooling rack, piping bag.

⚠ Get cooking

1. Heat the oven to 180°C (350°F/ Gas 4).
2. In a mixing bowl, add softened butter, egg, and syrup. Beat together with a wooden spoon until creamy.
3. Add the dry ingredients from the jar (except the sweets and icing sugar) and mix together well.
4. Use your hands to make the mixture into a ball. Wrap in cling film and leave in the fridge for 30 mins.
5. Roll out the mixture to 5mm (¼in) thickness. Cut out the cookies and place them on the baking tray.
6. Put in the oven and cook for 15 mins. Take out and allow to cool on a rack.
7. Decorate with icing and sweets.

FOR THE ICING
1. Put the icing sugar into a small bowl and add the lemon juice. Mix together and add a little water if too stiff.
2. Put into a piping bag ready to decorate.

Jars of goodies

for Doodlers

Make a giant pencil packed with all
a doodler needs to get creative.

Cut out a circle from
brown paper. Fold it
into a cone to fit the
top of the lid
(see page 61).

Colour in
the top of
the pencil.

Glue to the
lid with
strong glue.

for A sweetie

Dress up two jars and fill them with
someone's favourite treats.

Make a jolly
hat from an
old glove
(see page 60).

Cut off the
cuff and two
fingers of an
old glove. Sew
them together
to make a
cosy scarf.

Glue on
wobbly eyes,
a button
nose, and a
salt dough
smile.

Find out more about decorating the jars on page 60.

You will need:
- Clean glass (or good quality plastic) jars with screw-on lids

for Keen crafters

Here's a sewing kit for budding stitchers. They'll have all they need in one place, topped off with a pincushion.

Create a pincushion from a two-part lid (see page 60).

for Cookie cooks

Not only does this cookie jar contain ingredients and instructions for making delicious cookies, it even serves as a cookie container!

Ingredients:

150g (5½oz) soft brown sugar
225g (8oz) plain flour
1 tsp bicarbonate of soda
150g (5½oz) candy-coated sweets
(in a plastic bag)

Fill up the jar using the same method as on page 19.

Make a fancy label and write out the cooking instructions (see page 60).

Bathtime fizz

These bath fizzes are full of fizzy fun!
Watch them explode with delicious flowery scents as they
melt in the bath. They're the perfect gift for anyone who
deserves a relaxing time.

A treat just
for YOU
x

Sugar cake
decorations will
melt away in
the bath.

How to make a bath fizz

The basic recipe contains bicarbonate of soda, citric acid, oil, and water. You can change the colour, smell, decoration, and shape to suit the lucky recipient of your gift.

Lavender scented fizzers
You will need:

Blue food colouring

Lavender scented oil

100g (3½oz) citric acid

2 tsp olive oil

Sugar stars

Water sprayer

200g (7oz) bicarbonate of soda

- large mixing bowl • teaspoon
- large spoon for mixing
- ice-cube tray to make the shapes

1

Citric acid

Bicarbonate of soda

Olive oil

Combine the three ingredients (as shown) in the mixing bowl.

Mix it up

2

Food colouring

Stir the colour into the mixture.

Add some colour

3

Scented oil

Other scented oils to try: vanilla, peppermint, or orange.

Add about 10 drops of scented oil and mix well.

Add some nice smells

4 Spray about 7 squirts of water and mix in well.

Add water

5 The mixture is ready when it clumps together.

Try squeezing it together with your hands. ....

Shape the bath fizzers

Use a clean, dry ice-cube tray or similar mould.

1 Sprinkle sugar-star decorations into the shapes.

Ice-cube tray with heart shapes

2 Spoon in the mixture. Press it down and keep filling.

3 Firmly press down the mixture into the mould.

4 Leave to set for 2 hours, then pop out the fizzers.

Ready to gift wrap

Fill a clean, dry, air-tight jar.

Use within one month to make the most of the smells.

More fizzy ideas

Use the same basic mix, but try adding different scented oils or decorations. You can also use other moulds, such as bun tins.

Refreshing ice

You will need:
- ice-cube tray
- basic fizzy mix
- peppermint scented oil
- sparkly cake decorations

Tangy citrus cupcakes

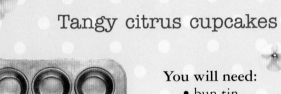

You will need:
- bun tin
- basic fizzy mix
- orange scented oil
- sugar cake decorations

Picture it!

Create a work of art for a special person. Draw a simple design
and fill in the shape to create a gem of a picture.

Buttons,
beads, and
googly
eyes

You will need:

Picture frame:
about 20cm x 20cm
(8in x 8in) is a good size

White paper

Thin card

Scissors

Strong glue

Pencil

1 Draw a simple shape on
paper and cut it out.

Place the paper shape
on the card, and trace
round it.

2 Cut out the card shape, and
position it on a piece of paper
that fits your frame. Lightly
draw round the shape.

3

Spread glue
inside the
shape.

Stick on googly eyes, then
starting at the edge, add
buttons and beads. Soon your
picture will be ready to frame!

You're a star!

Use a mini canvas for a pocket-sized picture.

Use felt-tip pens to add details to your design.

This belongs to…

Make your favourite people feel special with their very own decorated ceramics. This mug for Mum will be perfect for her well-earned tea breaks.

You can add a treat, too. Wrap it in a pretty bag tied with a ribbon.

Mum

You're all heart

Draw a picture or doodle some simple patterns.

You will need:

- plain, glazed ceramics
- porcelain pens • scissors • paper
- double-sided sticky tape or stickers

You can use any plain, glazed ceramics, such as cups, saucers, mugs, plates, or egg cups.

Purr-fect for cat lovers

A matching cat plate

Making pictures

1

Try out some designs first with pen and paper – just doodle!

2

Draw your design directly onto the ceramic surface.

3

Colour in your design, add a name, then leave to dry.

Mum

Scribbles and dots

1

Use stickers or paper stuck to double-sided sticky tape.

Cut out a shape.

2

Stick your shape on the mug. Draw some scribbles or dots.

3

Leave to dry, then peel off the shape.

Write a message.

You're the best!

To fix your design:

⚠️ 1. Place the dry items on an ovenproof tray.
2. Place the tray on the middle shelf in a COLD oven.
3. Heat the oven to 160°C (325°F/Gas 3).
4. Bake for 30 minutes, then turn off the oven.
5. ALLOW THE ITEMS TO COOL DOWN.
6. Remove them from the oven when cold.

NOTE: Follow the manufacturer's instructions given with your pens.

Not sure about drawing a picture? Then use a sticker shape and scribble over it (see instructions opposite).

Make a pincushion. Wrap fabric round soft stuffing, then glue the cushion into an egg cup.

Egg heads

Make a gift set

Once you are happy with your design, apply it to different ceramic things to make up a collection, such as a mug with a matching coaster and plate.

We're dotty about you

Top tile coasters

Decorate plain ceramic tiles and heat in the same way as the plates and cups.

Thanks a bunch

Paper roses are as pretty as the real ones, but by using paper petals and fuzzy pipe cleaners, there are no prickly thorns!

You will need:

Thin card discs

Colourful construction paper

Scissors

Pencil

Strong glue

Skewer with pointed tip

Pipe cleaners

Tip: Cut out different sized paper discs to make roses in a variety of sizes.

Everything's coming up roses!

Make them match

For the perfect matching gift set, make smaller roses and stick them onto a greetings card, a gift tag, and wrapping paper.

How to make a rose

1 Cut out a paper disc

Place a card disc on the coloured paper and draw round it with a pencil. Cut out the paper disc.

2 Turn the disc into a spiral

Draw a spiral on the paper disc, then cut it out.

Roll up at the outer end of the spiral.

Roll round the skewer.

3 Roll it up

Let the spiral open out slightly.

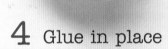

Glue the inner, flat end.

Stick the flat end and the coiled paper together.

4 Glue in place

Bend the tip of the pipe cleaner over to hold it in place.

Make a hole with a skewer through the base of the rose.

Insert the pipe cleaner through the hole to make the stalk.

5 Make a hole

6 Insert the stalk

Crafty
cards

Love bugs

Special greetings

are brought to you on the backs of these cute little critters. Flutter their wings to reveal the secret messages.

Glitter bug

Love bug

Use sparkly paper and shiny sticker stars.

Ladybirds are really cute, but you can make your bugs as unique as you like. Experiment with stickers and glittery paper.

Stripy bug

How to make a love bug card

You will need:

- colourful paper for body and wings
- scissors
- eraser
- paper fastener
- glue stick
- folded greetings card
- wobbly eyes
- felt-tip pens

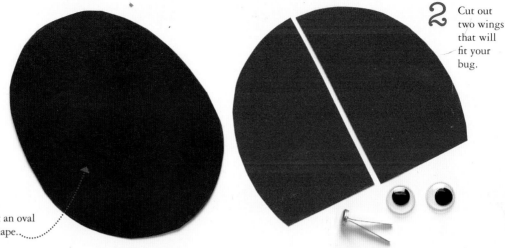

1 Cut out an oval body shape.

2 Cut out two wings that will fit your bug.

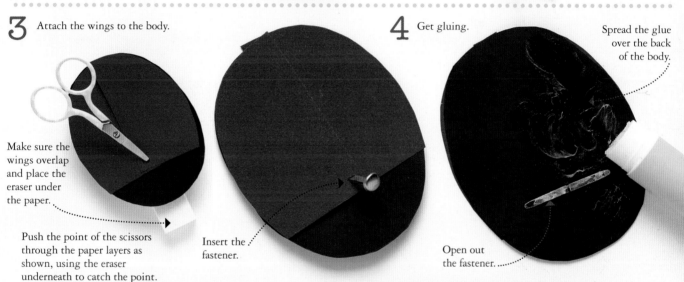

3 Attach the wings to the body.

Make sure the wings overlap and place the eraser under the paper.

Push the point of the scissors through the paper layers as shown, using the eraser underneath to catch the point.

Insert the fastener.

4 Get gluing.

Spread the glue over the back of the body.

Open out the fastener.

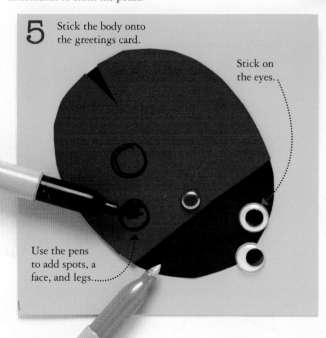

5 Stick the body onto the greetings card.

Stick on the eyes.

Use the pens to add spots, a face, and legs.

6 It's ready to add your message.

Add details such as eyelashes.

Pop-up greetings

Surprise surprise! Tell someone they're
special with these pop-up bouquets, beating hearts,
and stacks of gift boxes. Bring your paper pictures
to life with simple 3D effects.

Spring has sprung just for you in this gift card.

How to make cards pop

You will need:

Thin card 24cm x 17cm (9½in x 6½in)

Thick paper
23cm x 16cm
(9in x 6in)

Scissors

Glue stick

Pencil

Ruler

Scraps of paper or stickers

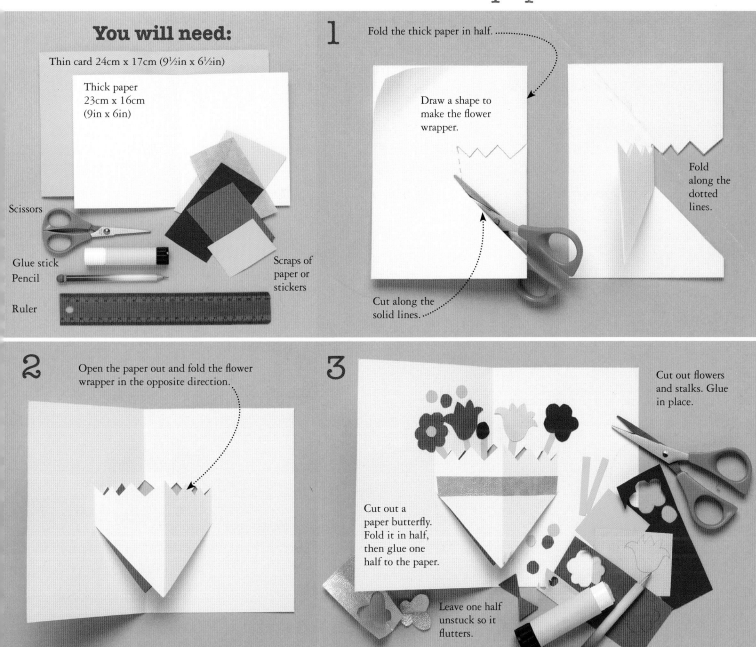

1 Fold the thick paper in half.

Draw a shape to make the flower wrapper.

Fold along the dotted lines.

Cut along the solid lines.

2 Open the paper out and fold the flower wrapper in the opposite direction.

3 Cut out flowers and stalks. Glue in place.

Cut out a paper butterfly. Fold it in half, then glue one half to the paper.

Leave one half unstuck so it flutters.

4 Make flowers for the front of the bouquet.

Glue to the inside of the flower wrapper.

5 Fold the outer thin card in half.

Glue the backs of the inner paper onto the outer thin card.

The front is ready to decorate with more flowers.

Close up the card, and press the layers together.

Pop-up hearts, cakes, and gifts

Big heart

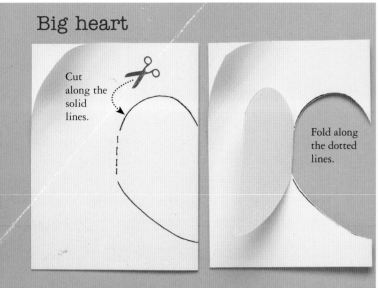

Cut along the solid lines.

Fold along the dotted lines.

Open the paper out. Fold the heart in the opposite direction.

Decorate with paper hearts.

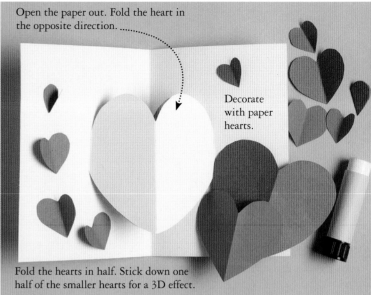

Fold the hearts in half. Stick down one half of the smaller hearts for a 3D effect.

Celebration cake

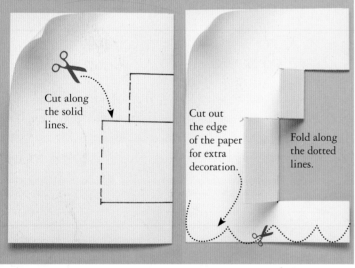

Cut along the solid lines.

Cut out the edge of the paper for extra decoration.

Fold along the dotted lines.

Open the paper out. Fold the cakes in the opposite direction.

Glue paper candles to the inside edge.

Stick on strips of paper for the icing.

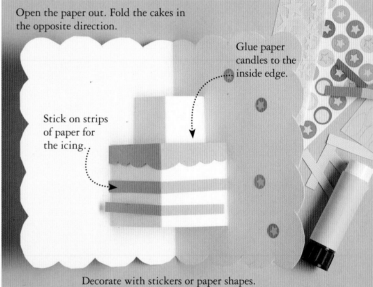

Decorate with stickers or paper shapes.

Gifts galore

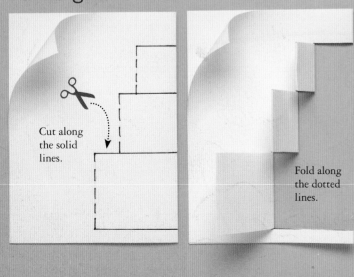

Cut along the solid lines.

Fold along the dotted lines.

Decorate the gifts with pretty paper. Cut out paper bows and stick them on.

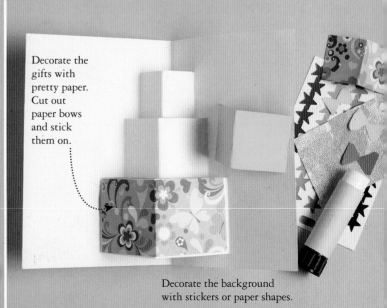

Decorate the background with stickers or paper shapes.

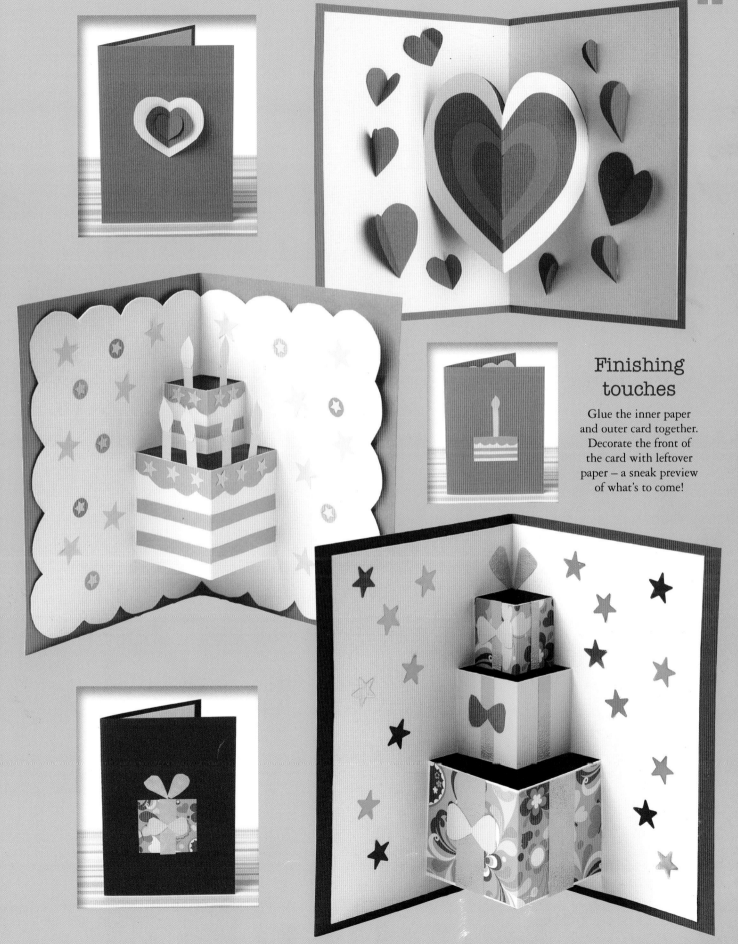

Finishing touches

Glue the inner paper and outer card together. Decorate the front of the card with leftover paper – a sneak preview of what's to come!

Snap happy

The kittens arrived.

When we baked you an apple pie.

They've seen a mouse.

Playing ball with

Choosing a new bed.

We jumped on

Remember when...
Share the times you visited friends,
got a new pet, or just had fun! Make a mini album
of photos you've taken and pack them up in this clever camera card.

Memory cards

To create a camera card, glue your favourite photos to a sheet of folded paper. Stick the folded paper inside a greetings card ready for the big reveal.

You will need:

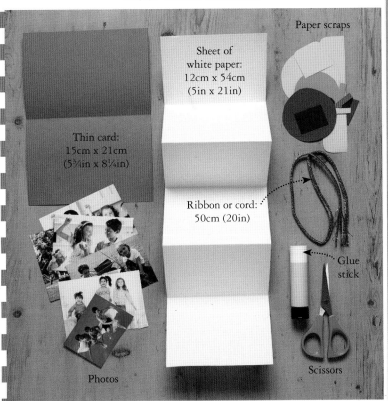

Thin card:
15cm x 21cm
(5¾in x 8¼in)

Sheet of
white paper:
12cm x 54cm
(5in x 21in)

Paper scraps

Ribbon or cord:
50cm (20in)

Glue
stick

Photos

Scissors

Decorate the front

1 Fold the card, then cut off the corners.

Cut out paper shapes to make the camera.

2 Glue the paper shapes in position.

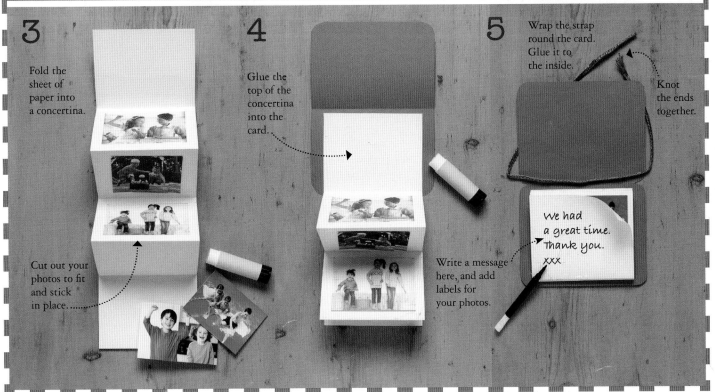

3 Fold the sheet of paper into a concertina.

Cut out your photos to fit and stick in place.

4 Glue the top of the concertina into the card.

5 Wrap the strap round the card. Glue it to the inside.

Knot the ends together.

Write a message here, and add labels for your photos.

We had a great time. Thank you. xxx

Cards for crafters

and grafters

Pack these hobby pouches with tools for a special crafter or grafter. They make ideal gifts for DIY experts, keen cooks, green-fingered gardeners, or those who love to sew.

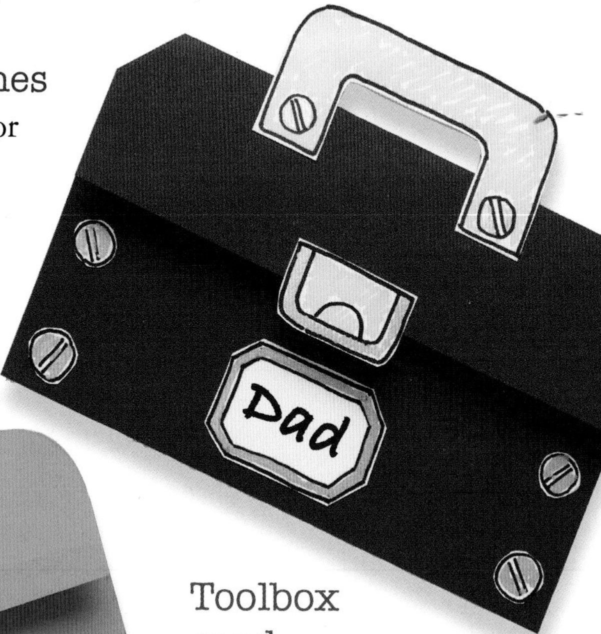

Toolbox card

Sewing box card

You will need:

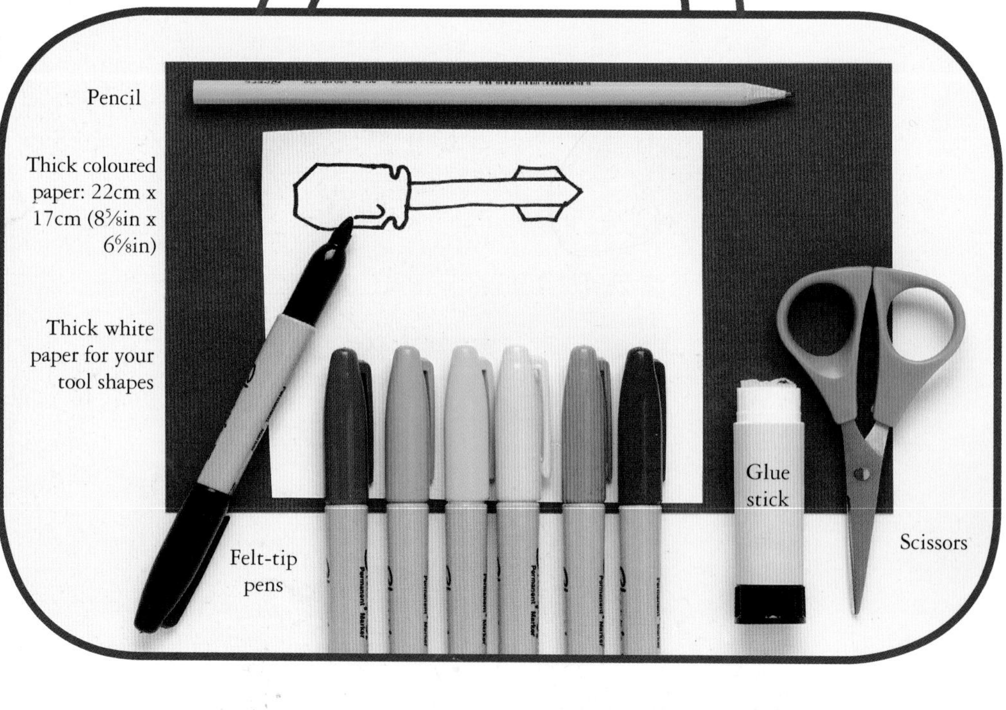

Pencil

Thick coloured paper: 22cm x 17cm (8⅝in x 6⅝in)

Thick white paper for your tool shapes

Felt-tip pens

Glue stick

Scissors

Dad

Alice

For the DIYers

Dad

Tools for
the job

Draw tool shapes
on white paper.
Colour them in,
cut them out,
and pop them
in the pouch.

Sew, it's your birthday!

Alice

For the
stitchers

Write the person's
name on the front,
and add a message
under the flap.

How to make a box card

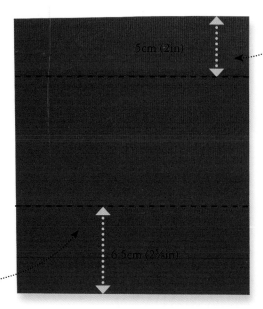

5cm (2in)

Fold the upper section inwards.

Only glue the edges of the bottom section, and stick to make the pocket.

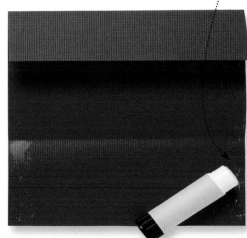

1 Fold the coloured paper along the black dotted lines.

Fold the lower section inwards.

6.5cm (2¾in)

2

Draw the tools with a pencil.

Go over the lines in felt-tip pen.

Cut out the tools and colour them in.

3

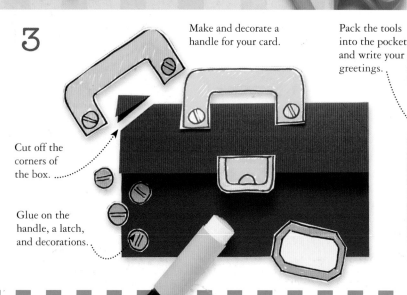

Make and decorate a handle for your card.

Pack the tools into the pocket and write your greetings.

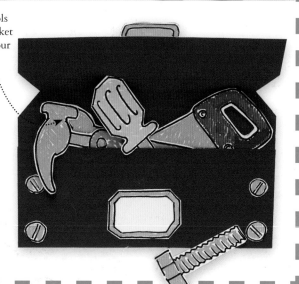

Cut off the corners of the box.

Glue on the handle, a latch, and decorations.

Crafty
Gift Wrap

Pillow boxes

A small gift is made extra special when it is presented in a neat little gift box. It's easy to make a pillow box from a cardboard tube.

You will need:

• cardboard tube • scissors • gift wrap or coloured paper • glue stick • ribbons • googly eyes

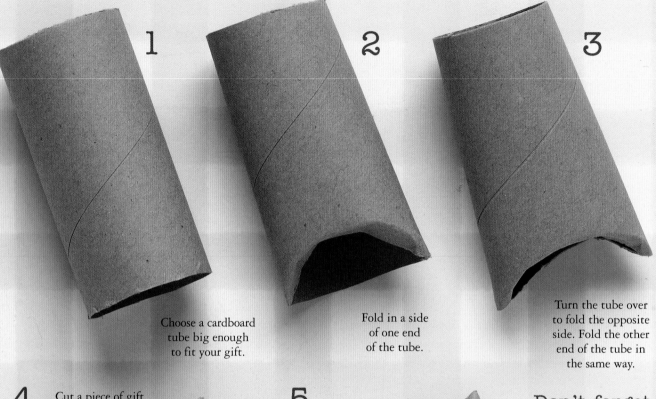

1 Choose a cardboard tube big enough to fit your gift.

2 Fold in a side of one end of the tube.

3 Turn the tube over to fold the opposite side. Fold the other end of the tube in the same way.

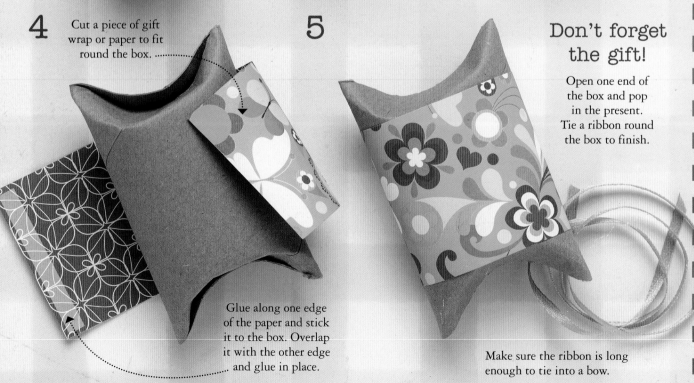

4 Cut a piece of gift wrap or paper to fit round the box.

5

Glue along one edge of the paper and stick it to the box. Overlap it with the other edge and glue in place.

Don't forget the gift!

Open one end of the box and pop in the present. Tie a ribbon round the box to finish.

Make sure the ribbon is long enough to tie into a bow.

Alien

One googly eye is all it takes!

Little boxes

Decorate your boxes with leftover gift wrap, paper, or ribbons. Or bring them to life with googly eyes.

Owl

Add paper wings and a paper triangle for a beak. Finish off with big googly eyes.

For terrific trinkets

Little

There's no need to buy fancy containers when giving gifts. Make your own cheap and cheerful cartons from plain paper plates.

boxes

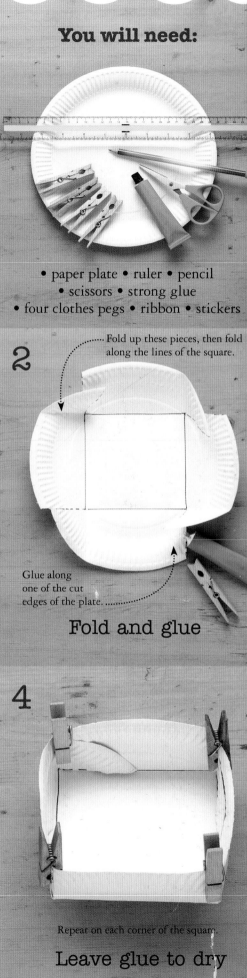

You will need:

• paper plate • ruler • pencil
• scissors • strong glue
• four clothes pegs • ribbon • stickers

2

Fold up these pieces, then fold along the lines of the square.

Glue along one of the cut edges of the plate.

Fold and glue

4

Repeat on each corner of the square.

Leave glue to dry

1

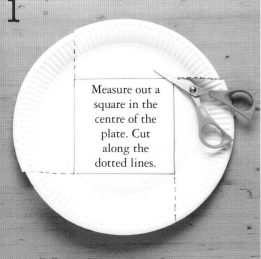

Measure out a square in the centre of the plate. Cut along the dotted lines.

Measure and cut

3

Place the next edge against the glued edge. Hold in place with a peg.

Peg corner in place

5

When dry, decorate with a ribbon and stickers.

Now decorate

Stacks of gifts

Fill the boxes with homemade cookies or load them up with someone's favourite sweets.

Flat packs

Wrap flat gifts such as gift tokens in these simple envelopes made from overlapping circles of colourful paper.

You will need:

- coloured paper (two different colours)
- glue stick • pencil
- scissors • ribbon

Circles and sizes

To make the circles, draw round something, such as a saucer or a lid from a jar.

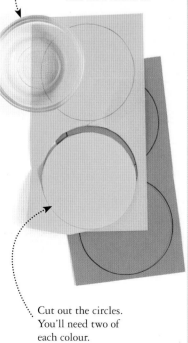

Place the circular object onto the paper and draw round it.

Cut out the circles. You'll need two of each colour.

How to make a flat pack

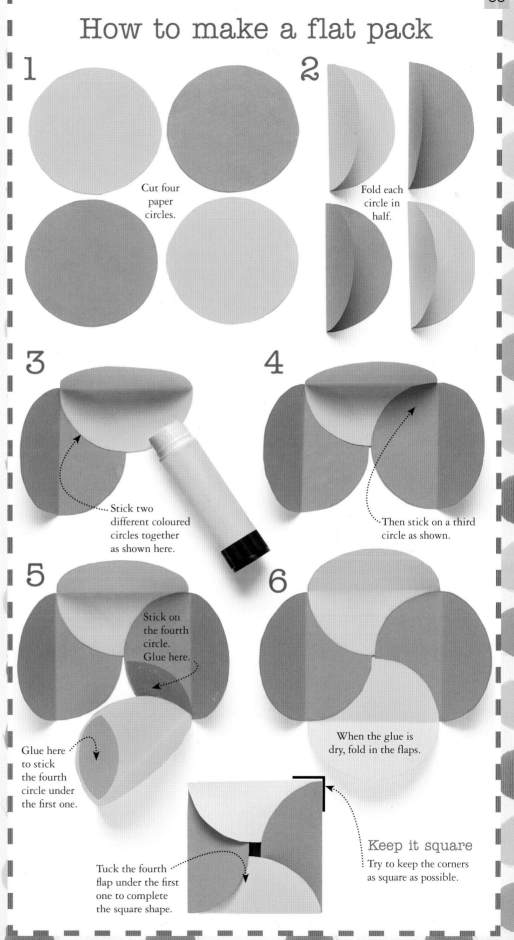

1 Cut four paper circles.

2 Fold each circle in half.

3 Stick two different coloured circles together as shown here.

4 Then stick on a third circle as shown.

5 Stick on the fourth circle. Glue here.

Glue here to stick the fourth circle under the first one.

6 When the glue is dry, fold in the flaps.

Tuck the fourth flap under the first one to complete the square shape.

Keep it square
Try to keep the corners as square as possible.

Brown paper packages

Transform plain old brown paper by adding faces, stickers, and painted patterns to your parcels.

The three bears

Brown boxes become Dad, Mum, and Baby Bear with the addition of ears, wobbly eyes, and white paper muzzles (see page 59).

A treat just for You!

Dot to dotty

Polka dots and wavy line designs can be made from simple stickers.

The reindeer

Pipe cleaners bent into antler shapes turn these parcels into reindeer (see page 59).

Pom-pommed

Use strong glue to attach ready-made pom-poms.

Cosy kids

Recycle snack tubes and turn them into characters with funny faces. Add woolly hats made from socks or gloves (see page 60).

DIY gift wrap

Print shop

Design your own colourful gift wrap. Using household items, print shapes onto plain brown paper, and create exotic patterns like these.

Diamonds and dots

Funny honeycomb

Crinkly circles

Luscious gold

Daisies

Latticework

You will need:

- sheets of brown paper • sticky tape • acrylic paint • paintbrush
- plate for paint • household items to make prints • plain gift tags

Plastic bag

Crumple up a plastic bag and simply press it into the paint. Then apply to the paper.

Cookie cutter

Dip the cutter into the paint, then press it onto the paper. Overlap the shapes to make an interlocking design.

Prepare to print

Take a sheet of paper. Lay it on a flat surface and tape down the corners.

Cover the paper with the print design and leave to dry before wrapping.

Pencil erasers

Tape seven pencils together, making sure the ends are lined up to make an even print.

Don't forget to print matching gift tags and cards.

Pencil eraser

Single pencils make spotty designs.

Toothbrush

Bubble wrap

Cut out a piece of bubble wrap. Press it into the paint, then apply it to the paper to print bubbles.

Paint

Spread a thick layer of paint over the plate with a paintbrush. Press the items for printing into the paint, then apply them to the paper. Add more paint as needed.

All wrapped up

Wrap your gifts like a professional,
then add your printed tags.

You will need:

- printed gift wrap paper
  and gift tags
- scissors
- sticky tape
- ribbons

Tip for a neat wrap

Don't use too much paper
or your folds will be bulky.
Use just enough to cover
your box.

1 Lay the box in the
middle of the paper.

2 Wrap the paper round
the box, folding along
the edges as shown.

3 Overlap
the paper,
then tape it
together.

4 Fold down one
end as shown.

5 Fold one
side in towards
the box.

6 Fold the
other side in, then press
down the creases.

7 Fold the
triangular end up
and tape it in place.

8 Do the same
to the other end
of the box. Add a
ribbon to finish.

Bear face

You will need:

• brown, pink, and white paper • scissors • glue stick • strong glue • googly eyes • felt-tip pen • buttons • ribbon

Add a bow and buttons to make it look like the bear is wearing a shirt.

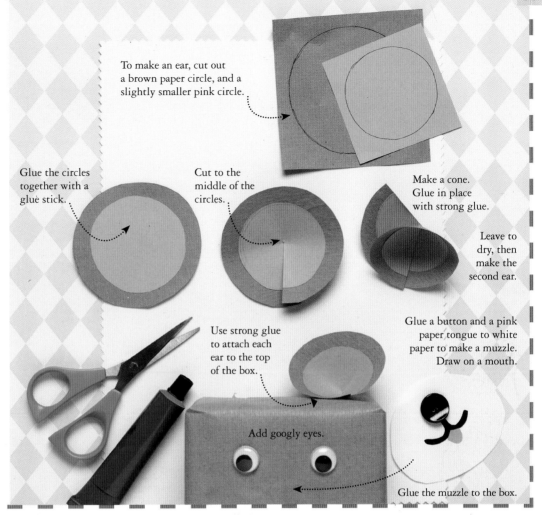

To make an ear, cut out a brown paper circle, and a slightly smaller pink circle.

Glue the circles together with a glue stick.

Cut to the middle of the circles.

Make a cone. Glue in place with strong glue.

Leave to dry, then make the second ear.

Glue a button and a pink paper tongue to white paper to make a muzzle. Draw on a mouth.

Use strong glue to attach each ear to the top of the box.

Add googly eyes.

Glue the muzzle to the box.

Ears and antlers

You will need:

• scissors • brown and pink paper • glue stick • two brown pipe cleaners • sticky tape

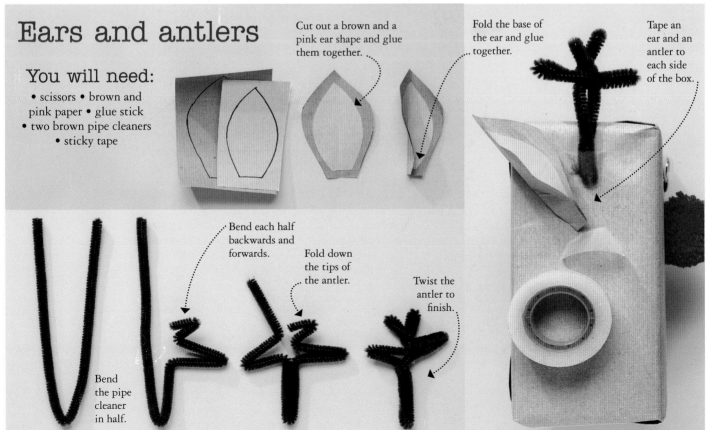

Cut out a brown and a pink ear shape and glue them together.

Fold the base of the ear and glue together.

Tape an ear and an antler to each side of the box.

Bend the pipe cleaner in half.

Bend each half backwards and forwards.

Fold down the tips of the antler.

Twist the antler to finish.

Cosy kids
Make a beany hat from a glove.

You will need:
• Woollen glove • elastic band • needle and cotton thread • pom-pom

Turn a woollen glove inside out.

Gather it up with an elastic band.

Turn it right side out. (You can leave the fingers inside.)

Sew on a pom-pom.

Stretch the hat over the package and adjust to fit.

Cookie cooks
Here's how you make these delicious cookies.

Make a label for the cooking instructions.

Write the instructions here.

Makes: 20 cookies

You will also need:
• 150g (5½oz) softened butter
• 1 tbsp milk

Equipment: mixing bowl • wooden spoon • metal spoon • baking tray • cooling rack

Get cooking
1. Heat the oven to 190°C (375°F/Gas 5).
2. Add the dry ingredients from the jar and mix together well with the butter and milk.
3. Mix in the sweets.
4. Make the mixture into 20 balls of dough.
5. Place on the baking tray and flatten the balls with the back of a spoon.
6. Put in the oven and cook for 15 mins. Take out and allow to cool on a rack.

Keen crafter
Make a handy pincushion lid.

You will need:

Needle and thread

Scissors

Jar with a two-part screw lid

Soft stuffing

Strong glue

A disc of cotton fabric (large enough to fold over the stuffing and the lid)

Tip: Place the stuffing into a nylon sock so that it will hold its shape.

1

Place the ball of stuffing in the centre of the fabric.

Put this part of the lid on top with the base facing out.

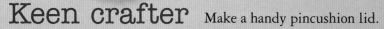

Doodler's kit

Make a giant pencil jar.

You will need: • thick brown paper • pencil • plate • black pen • scissors • strong glue • paper clip or other paper fastener

1
Draw round a plate to make a circle on the brown paper.

2
Cut out the paper circle.

Cut into the centre.

Twist the paper to form a cone.

3
Check the cone will fit the top of your jar.

Hold the cone in place with a clip while you stick it with strong glue. Leave the cone to dry.

4
Apply strong glue to the top of the lid, round the edge.

Hold the pencil top in position until the glue has dried.

5
Colour in the tip of the pencil top with black pen.

Once the glue has dried, remove the lid. Fill the jar with gifts, then decorate.

2
Bring the fabric over the lid. Gather it up and stitch together.

3
Apply strong glue to the inside rim of the lid (not the screw part).

Push the cushion through the opening of the lid.

Stitch the fabric together tightly and secure the end of the thread.

4
Place the lid on top of the jar and screw it up tightly.

Allow the glue to dry, then open the jar and fill it with your gift.

Index